GIFTS OF

CHRISTMAS

Sights and Sounds

of the Season

TYNDALE HOUSE PUBLISHERS, INC ✳ WHEATON, ILLINOIS

Visit Tyndale's exciting Web site at www.tyndale.com

Gifts of Christmas: Sights and Sounds of the Season copyright © 2000 by Tyndale House Publishers, Inc., Wheaton, Illinois 60189. All rights reserved.

Cover photograph by Ric Ergenbright

Photography by Ric Ergenbright

Development Director Tammy Faxel

Designed by Gloria Chantell

Devotions written by Erin Keeley

"The Promise of the Doll" by Ruth C. Ikerman. Text reprinted by permission of Joe Wheeler, editor/compiler of *Christmas in My Heart*, vol. 1 (Conifer, Colorado) and Christian Herald, Inc.

"Two Babes in a Manger." Author and original source unknown. Efforts were made to secure permission to reprint this story. If anyone can provide information about this story's origins, please contact Tyndale House Publishers, Inc.

"Waiting, Waiting for Christmas" by Elizabeth King English. Reprinted with permission from *Guideposts* magazine (Dec. 1983). Copyright © 1983 by Guideposts, Carmel, New York 10512.

"The Manger Was Empty" retold by Casandra Lindell. Original author and source unknown. Used by permission of Casandra Lindell.

"Trouble at the Inn" by Dina Donohue. Reprinted with permission from *Guideposts* magazine. Copyright © 1966 by Guideposts, Carmel, New York 10512.

"And for as Long as I Can Remember" by Catherine Otten. Efforts were made to secure permission to reprint this story. If anyone can provide current copyright information, please contact Tyndale House Publishers, Inc.

Adapted from "The Dime." Author and original source unknown. If anyone can provide information about this story's origins, please contact Tyndale House Publishers, Inc.

"Christmas Is for Love." Author and original source unknown. If anyone can provide information about this story's origins, please contact Tyndale House Publishers, Inc. Reprinted by www.arlenes-heavenlywebs.com

"The Doll and a White Rose" by V. A. Bailey. Original copyright and source unknown. If anyone can provide information about this story's origins, please contact Tyndale House Publishers, Inc. Reprinted by www.arlenes-heavenlywebs.com

"Unexpected Christmas" by Marguerite Nixon. Original copyright © 1965 by *Weekly Unity*. (Reprinted in *Christmas in My Heart*, vol. 7, copyright © 1998 by Joe L. Wheeler. Published by Tyndale House Publishers, Inc., Wheaton, Illinois 60189.) Efforts were made to secure permission to reprint this story. If anyone can provide current copyright information, please contact Tyndale House Publishers, Inc.

Scripture quotations are taken from the *Holy Bible*, New Living Translation, copyright © 1996. Used by permission of Tyndale House Publishers, Inc., Wheaton, Illinois 60189. All rights reserved.

ISBN 0-8423-4242-7

Printed in China

04	03	02	01	00
5	4	3	2	1

CONTENTS

INTRODUCTION

Christmas is like no other time of year. For weeks in advance, people everywhere spend hours preparing for that most-special day. Thoughts are filled with visions of gifts to be given and those to be received, whose list is longest, and whose will stretch the budget the most.

The holiday began two thousand years ago with a gift, so it's naturally fitting that the tradition has continued. God's gift of life—his Son, Jesus—will always be the most precious one any of us can receive. He is the true "Gift that keeps on giving," for only through him can we experience genuine peace and unreserved joy.

Gifts of Christmas: Sights and Sounds of the Season is a celebration of the many intangible blessings we have in God. Beautiful images are blended with favorite old carols, traditions, Scriptures, and stories in this timeless collection. In the pages that follow, allow your heart to be drawn to the deeper meaning of the holiday. Take with you the truths about love, freedom, comfort, and refreshment; then offer them to your loved ones this Christmas.

Wherever you are and whatever your plans, may you revel in the many unspoken gifts of the season!

I

WRITE A LIST OF PEOPLE YOU'RE THANKFUL FOR; PRAY

FOR ONE PERSON EACH DAY OF DECEMBER—

GIVE YOUR HEART DURING THE SEASON OF GIVING.

Christ's perfect life was the perfect manifestation

of human life as God intended it.

SOURCE UNKNOWN

CHAPTER I

The Gift of Life

O LITTLE TOWN OF BETHLEHEM

Phillips Brooks, 1868

O little town of Bethlehem,

How still we see thee lie!

Above thy deep and dreamless sleep

The silent stars go by.

Yet in thy dark streets shineth

The everlasting light;

The hopes and fears of all the years

Are met in thee tonight.

For Christ is born of Mary,

And gathered all above,

While mortals sleep, the angels keep

Their watch of wond'ring love.

O morning stars, together

Proclaim the holy birth,

And praises sing to God the King,

And peace to men on earth.

How silently, how silently

The wondrous gift is given!

So God imparts to human hearts

The blessings of His heaven.

No ear may hear His coming,

But in this world of sin,

Where meek souls will receive Him, still

The dear Christ enters in.

O holy Child of Bethlehem

Descend to us, we pray;

Cast out our sin, and enter in,

Be born in us today.

We hear the Christmas angels

The great glad tidings tell;

O come to us, abide with us,

Our Lord Emmanuel!

CHRISTMASTIME BRINGS WITH IT a variety of emotions: exhilaration and anticipation; gratitude and compassion; weariness and even some loneliness. Some years are full of blessings, while other times the holiday seems less festive. That's life—ups and downs blended together.

Fortunately, there is one truth we can rely on no matter what: God always has been and always will remain good. His character is unchanging. He is the same today as he was on that first Christmas when he sent his Son, Jesus, to earth as a tiny baby so that he could eventually give his life for all people. So great is God's compassion that he would have sent Jesus if only one of us had needed him. His life changed ours.

That's the message of "O Little Town of Bethlehem": new life. God's people had waited hundreds of years for the Messiah who would save them. That beautiful moment in a small village outside Jerusalem forever altered eternity. Stop and think about that in a fresh way this year. He was born for you.

God wants more for your life than you could ever imagine. What an incredible gift he's given us!

5

MY PURPOSE IS TO GIVE LIFE IN ALL ITS FULLNESS.

JOHN 10:10

The Promise of the Doll

BY RUTH C. IKERMAN

When I met my friend on the crowded street, she held out her hand to me and said, "I hope you can help me. I'm desperate." Wearily she explained, "I'm about to cry and it's all over a doll. I simply have to find this doll for my grand-daughter."

As tears filled her eyes, I remembered the terrible shock we all had felt over the death of her daughter, who had been such a vivacious young mother until stricken several months before. The young husband was doing a fine job with the little girl, but it was on the grandmother that much of the burden of planning for good things remained. And this explained her Christmas errand.

"I blame myself entirely," she told me, "for not starting earlier, but I never thought it would be a problem to find one of these special dolls. Yet there is not one of this variety left in town."

I asked her, "Well, why can't you settle for another kind of doll?"

She shook her head. "One of the last things my daughter ever said to me before the pain got so bad was how sorry she was that she had refused to buy this doll for her little girl. She told me she had thought the child was too young for such a doll, and had refused to buy it for her birthday, supposing there were lots of occasions ahead when she could get it for her."

Then she told the rest of the story. The little girl had come to her mother's bedside and asked whether the doll might arrive at Christmastime. The young mother grasped the tiny hand in hers and said, "I promise you this for Christmas." Then she had asked her own mother to do this one thing: "Just make sure that my little girl gets that doll this Christmas."

Now my friend was about to fail in her mission. "It's all my fault," she kept repeating. "I waited until too late. It will take a miracle now."

Secretly I agreed, but I tried to keep up a polite facade of courage. "Maybe the child has forgotten and will be happy with something else."

Grimly my friend replied, "*She* may forget, but *I* won't."
We parted to go our separate ways.

With my mind only half on my shopping, I found
the ribbon a neighbor wanted to finish a baby blanket she was
making. A few minutes later I stopped at her door to leave the
package and was invited inside.

Her two little girls sat on the floor, playing with their
dolls. As I sat down, I noticed that one of the dolls was the
same type my friend was seeking. Hopefully I asked, "Can you
remember where you bought that doll?"

My neighbor gave me her warmhearted smile. "That's not
a doll," she said, "she's a member of the family, and as near as I
can see she probably was born and not made. She came to us by
plane from a favorite aunt in the East."

So I told her that I had a friend who was searching franti-
cally for such a doll for the little girl whose mother had passed
away during the year. Apparently unaware of us, the two children
played happily. The mother and I spoke in adult words about

facing loss at the holiday time, and how much we wished we could help my friend.

Later when I got up to leave, the two little girls followed me to the door.

"Dolly is ready to leave, too," they told me. Sure enough, she was dressed in a red velveteen coat and hat with a white fur muff.

"Where is dolly going?" I asked.

They laughed happily. "With you, of course. You know where the lady lives, don't you-the one who needs the doll so bad?"

I started to tell them that of course I couldn't take this doll. Then I looked at their faces, happy in the moment of giving. If I say the wrong thing now, something within my heart warned, I may ruin their joy of giving for the rest of their lives. Silently I took the doll, fumbling with my car keys so that they would not see the mist over my eyes.

Their mother asked, "Are you both sure you want to do this?" They answered, "Yes, we do . . ." The mother put her arms around them tenderly.

Later I rang the doorbell of my friend. "Don't ask me how I got it, for I can't talk just yet. The doll is a little smudgy, but the worn places are from kisses and maybe they won't show under the Christmas lights."

She cuddled the doll as though it were made of precious metal. Tears of joy welled up in the woman's eyes when I finally was able to tell the story.

"How can I ever thank those children enough?" she asked.

"They already have received a blessing greater than anything you or I could give them," I told her. "I saw their faces when they offered me the doll to bring to you."

And it was true. In the moment of giving they had also received, in ways past our finding out. A miracle had taken place. A promise could be kept, linking here with there, in the eternal circle of love of which the great gift of Christmas itself is a part. ✤

Dear Lord,

in this Christmas season may I reflect to others

the abundant grace you have shown me

by giving your life in place of mine.

Amen.

＊

GOD SO LOVED THE WORLD

THAT HE GAVE HIS ONLY SON, SO THAT EVERYONE

WHO BELIEVES IN HIM WILL NOT PERISH

BUT HAVE ETERNAL LIFE.

JOHN 3:16

MAKE A CANDLE WITH YOUR FAMILY (WAX GRAINS AND A WICK IN A SMALL JAR). COMMIT TO EAT DINNER TOGETHER AS MANY NIGHTS OF DECEMBER AS POSSIBLE, BURNING THE CANDLE EACH NIGHT. IF YOU ARE SINGLE, BURN IT EACH NIGHT AS YOU PRAY FOR A WORLD NEED.

The Son of God became a man to enable men to become sons of God.

C. S. LEWIS

CHAPTER 2

The Gift of Hope

O HOLY NIGHT

M. Cappeau de Roquemaure

O Holy Night!

The stars are brightly shining,

It is the night of the dear Savior's birth;

Long lay the world in sin and error pining,

Till He appeared and the soul felt its worth.

A thrill of hope, the weary world rejoices,

For yonder breaks a new and glorious morn;

Fall on your knees,

Oh, hear the angel voices!

O night divine,

O night when Christ was born!

O night, O holy night, O night divine!

Truly He taught us to love one another;

His law is love, and His gospel is peace.

Chains shall He break, for the slave is our brother,

And in His name all oppression shall cease.

Sweet hymns of joy in grateful chorus raise we,

Let all within us praise His holy name!

Christ is the Lord! O praise His name forever!

His power and glory evermore proclaim!

HOPE. WITHOUT IT THE WORLD would crumble, and the human heart would cease to beat. Throughout history, amidst times of peace and seasons of excruciating sufferings, hope is one enduring theme that exists to the end.

Yet, what is true hope based upon? Perhaps a better question is, Who is its source? One can hope for an eternity that all hunger will one day be abolished, that each person will live in safety, or that good will eventually triumph over evil. But at the end of the day, the value of our hope is entirely dependent on the reliability and faithfulness of the one we hope in.

The message of "O Holy Night" is the realization of a thrilling new era—an era that speaks of eternal life and restoration of fellowship between corrupt humanity and the almighty God of the universe. For thousands of years before, generation upon generation had placed their hope in the Messiah—the Savior who would free them.

At last that most holy night came, and, as the songwriter states, "A thrill of hope, the weary world rejoices, for yonder breaks a new and glorious morn!"

LORD, YOU KNOW THE HOPES OF THE HELPLESS.

SURELY YOU WILL LISTEN TO THEIR CRIES AND COMFORT THEM.

PSALM 10:17

Adapted from "Two Babes in a Manger"

AUTHOR UNKNOWN

In 1994, two Americans answered an invitation from the Russian Department of Education to teach morals and ethics (based on biblical principles) in public schools, prisons, businesses, the fire and police departments, and a large orphanage. About 100 boys and girls who had been abandoned, abused, and left in the care of a government-run program were in the orphanage. They relate the following story in their own words:

It was nearing the holiday season—time for our orphans to hear the Christmas story for the first time. We told them about Mary and Joseph arriving in Bethlehem. Finding no room in the inn, the couple went to a stable, where the baby Jesus was born and placed in a manger.

Throughout the story, the children and orphanage staff sat in amazement as they listened. Some sat on the edges of their stools, trying to grasp every word. Completing the story, we gave the children three small pieces of cardboard to make a crude manger. Each child was given a small paper square.

Following instructions, the children tore the paper and carefully laid strips in the manger for straw. Small squares of flannel were used for the baby's blanket, and a doll-like baby was cut from tan felt.

The orphans were busy assembling their manger as I walked among them to see if they needed any help. All went well until I got to one table where little Misha sat. He looked to be about 6 years old and had finished his project. As I looked at the little boy's manger, I was startled to see not one, but two babies in the manger. Quickly, I called for the translator to ask the lad about the two babies. Crossing his arms in front of him and looking at this completed manger scene, the child began to repeat the story very seriously.

For such a young boy, who had only heard the Christmas story once, he related the happenings accurately—until he came to the part where Mary put the baby Jesus in the manger.

Then Misha started to ad-lib his own ending to the

story as he said, "And when Maria laid the baby in the manger, Jesus looked at me and asked me if I had a place to stay. I told him I have no mamma and I have no papa, so I don't have any place to stay. Then Jesus told me I could stay with him. But I told him I couldn't, because I didn't have a gift to give him like everybody else did. But I wanted to stay with Jesus so much, so I thought about what I had that maybe I could use for a gift. I thought maybe if I kept him warm, that would be a good gift.

"So I asked Jesus, 'If I keep you warm, will that be a good enough gift?' And Jesus told me, 'If you keep me warm, that will be the best gift anybody ever gave me.'

"So I got into the manger, and then Jesus looked at me and he told me I could stay with him—for always."

As little Misha finished his story, his eyes brimmed full of tears that splashed down his little cheeks. The little orphan had found someone who would never abandon nor abuse him, someone who would stay with him—*for always*. ❈

Thank you, Father,

for the boundless hope you offer to us.

May we sense in ever-increasing ways the importance of Jesus'

birth and all it means for us today and for eternity.

In Jesus' name, amen.

✳

YOU FAITHFULLY ANSWER OUR PRAYERS

WITH AWESOME DEEDS, O GOD OUR SAVIOR. YOU ARE

THE HOPE OF EVERYONE ON EARTH.

PSALM 65:5

TAKE A WALK AROUND YOUR NEIGHBORHOOD; ASK GOD

TO BLESS AND GUIDE EACH HOME AS YOU PASS IT.

Happy, happy Christmas, that can win us back to the

delusions of our childhood days, recall to the old man

the pleasures of his youth, and transport the traveler

back to his own fireside and quiet home!

CHARLES DICKENS

CHAPTER 3

The Gift of Guidance

WE THREE KINGS

John Henry Hopkins, 1857

We three kings of Orient are;

Bearing gifts we traverse afar,

Field and fountain, moor and mountain,

Following yonder star.

O star of wonder, star of night,

Star with royal beauty bright,

Westward leading, still proceeding,

Guide us to thy perfect light.

Born a King on Bethlehem's plain,

Gold I bring to crown Him again,

King forever, ceasing never

Over us all to reign.

Glorious now behold Him arise,

King and God and Sacrifice;

Alleluia, alleluia!

Earth to heav'n replies.

HAVE YOU EVER WONDERED WHAT the wise men felt as they traveled the long distance to see the baby Jesus? What were they doing at the precise moment they first received the message to search for the new King?

Many times we walk unknowingly into the most miraculous events of our lives. Some may attribute those "coincidences" to chance or fate. However, there was a much more powerful and deliberate source guiding the wise men toward their young Savior. The Master and Creator of the universe had mapped out a plan generations before—a plan that included them in history's most blessed event.

God's guidance is available in the same powerful way today to anyone with a tender heart who seeks his hand along life's journey. What an experience the wise men would have missed had they closed their souls to discovering the one who would alter the eternal destiny of humankind.

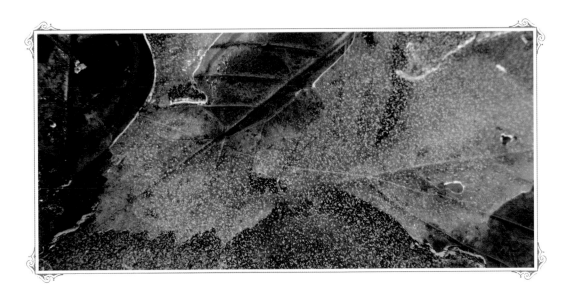

JESUS SAID TO THE PEOPLE, "I AM THE LIGHT OF THE WORLD. IF YOU FOLLOW ME, YOU WON'T BE STUMBLING THROUGH THE DARK-NESS, BECAUSE YOU WILL HAVE THE LIGHT THAT LEADS TO LIFE."

JOHN 8:12

Waiting, Waiting for Christmas

BY ELIZABETH KING ENGLISH

Herman and I locked our general store and dragged ourselves home. It was 11:00 P.M., Christmas Eve 1949. We were dog tired. We had sold almost all of our toys; and all of the layaways, except one package, had been picked up.

Usually we kept the store open until everything had been claimed. We wouldn't have woken up happy on Christmas knowing that some child's gift was still on the layaway shelf. But the person who had put a dollar down on that package never returned.

Early Christmas morning we and our twelve-year-old son, Tom, opened gifts. But I'll tell you, there was something humdrum about this Christmas. Tom was growing up; I missed his childish exuberance of past years.

As soon as breakfast was over Tom left to visit his friend next door. Herman mumbled, "I'm going back to sleep. There's nothing left to stay up for." So there I was alone, feeling let down.

And then it began. A strange, persistent urge. It seemed to be telling me to go to the store. I looked at the sleet and icy sidewalk outside. *That's crazy,* I said to myself. I tried dismissing the urge, but it wouldn't leave me alone. In fact, it was getting stronger. Finally, I couldn't stand it any longer, and I got dressed.

Outside, the wind cut right through me and the sleet stung my cheeks. I groped my way to the store, slipping and sliding. In front stood two boys, one about nine, and the other six. *What in the world?*

"See, I told you she would come!" the older boy said jubilantly. The younger one's face was wet with tears, but when he saw me, his sobbing stopped.

"What are you two doing here?" I scolded, hurrying them into the store. "You should be at home on a day like this!"

They were poorly dressed—no hats or gloves, and their shoes barely held together. I rubbed their icy hands and got them up close to the heater.

"We've been waiting for you," replied the older boy. "My little brother Jimmy didn't get any Christmas." He touched Jimmy's shoulder. "We want to buy some skates. That's what he wants. We have these three dollars," he said, pulling the bills from his pocket.

I looked at the money. I looked at their expectant faces. And then I looked around the store. "I'm sorry," I said, "but we have no—"

Then my eye caught sight of the layaway shelf with its lone package. "Wait a minute," I told the boys. I walked over, picked up the package, unwrapped it, and, miracle of miracles, there was a pair of skates!

Jimmy reached for them as I silently prayed, *Lord, let them be his size.* And miracle upon miracle, they *were* his size.

The older boy presented the dollars to me. "No," I told him, "I want you to have these skates, and I want you to use your money to get some gloves." The boys just blinked at first. Then their eyes became like saucers, and their grins stretched wide when they understood I was giving them the skates. What I saw in Jimmy's eyes was a blessing. It was pure joy, and it was beautiful. My spirits rose.

We walked out together, and as I locked the door, I turned to the older brother and said, "How did you know I would come?"

I wasn't prepared for his reply. His gaze was steady, and he answered me softly. "I asked Jesus to send you."

The tingles in my spine weren't from the cold. God had planned this. As we waved good-bye, I turned home to a brighter Christmas. ❈

Lord God,

thank you for your precious gift of eternal life.

Guide us each day of our lives,

and help us remember to seek the things that please you.

*

THE LORD HIMSELF WILL GUIDE YOU.

MICAH 2:13

IN A SMALL POT, PLANT SOME SEEDS OF A FAVORITE

HERB; ENJOY WATCHING THEM GROW DURING THE COLD

WINTER MONTHS AHEAD.

Dearer than memory, brighter than expectation

is the ever returning now of Christmas.

ELIZABETH BOWEN

CHAPTER 4

The Gift of Anticipation

O COME, O COME EMMANUEL

Latin, Ninth Century

O come, O come Emmanuel,

And ransom captive Israel,

That mourns in lonely exile here

Until the Son of God appear.

Rejoice, rejoice! Emmanuel

Shall come to thee, O Israel.

O come, Thou Dayspring, come and cheer

Our spirits by Thine advent here;

Disperse the gloomy clouds of night,

And death's dark shadows put to flight.

O come, Thou Key of David, come,

And open wide our heavenly home;

Make safe the way that leads on high,

And close the path to misery.

ONE OF THE MOST TREASURED qualities of the Christmas season is *anticipation*. For weeks ahead of time, hearts everywhere reflect the glow of expectation, knowing that wonderful happenings are right around the corner.

From our vantage point, the first Christmas seems eons ago. Think for a moment, though, what it might have been like to live *before* Jesus' birth. What an awesome sense of anticipation those days and years must have held for so many people who lived each moment awaiting the promised Messiah.

"O Come, O Come Emmanuel" brings to life the longing of a nation—the longing for freedom and healing—not so very different from the yearnings of today.

Whatever you have been waiting for or hoping to find, set your mind on the true meaning of the holiday. Nothing else measures up to the joy of knowing Jesus.

ALL CREATION ANTICIPATES THE DAY WHEN IT WILL JOIN GOD'S CHILDREN IN GLORIOUS FREEDOM FROM DEATH AND DECAY.

ROMANS 8:21

The Manger Was Empty

RETOLD BY CASANDRA LINDELL

He arrived early on Christmas morning to give the church a thorough inspection, noting with approval that the aisles and seats had been swept and dusted after the midnight Christmas Eve service. Any lost purses, Bibles, and gloves had been collected and sent to the office where the lost and found box was kept; every forgotten flyer and bulletin insert had been rounded up and discarded.

Outside it was just beginning to grow light. In the church, where only the pastor moved, candles flickered and threw shifting shadows on the arches and the stone floor. Occasionally, stray candlelight picked out the rich colors in the stained glass windows. It was cold and, except for the pastor's slow tread, it was silent.

He paused beside the almost life-sized nativity scene to say a Christmas prayer of thanksgiving to the One whose birth was being celebrated. The figures, each lovingly crafted with wonderful realism, sat on a small stage. A night sky and the star that had led the shepherds and the wise men to the Messiah on the day of His birth could be seen through the open door of the stable. The shepherds were just entering, eyes wide in obvious awe. Various kinds of livestock stood in stalls or lay on the edges of the scene. And in the center was the Holy Family. Looking at the manger scene, the pastor could almost feel the reverence of that night long ago.

Slowly, a puzzled frown crept across his brow. Then his choked gasp rustled through the empty church. The manger was empty! The small figure representing the infant Savior was gone.

Hurriedly, and with growing agitation, the pastor began to search the church. Starting by the manger, he peered back through the aisles, nearly crawling on his hands and knees to see all the way under each seat. But there was nothing. Next, he called the custodian, thinking *he* may have seen the figure of the infant Jesus. He called the assistant pastor and all the elders, but no one had any explanation. In the end, each shaking his head sorrowfully, they accepted the truth they had all been trying to avoid: The figure could not have been mislaid or lost— it must

have been stolen.

  With solemnity befitting the occasion, the pastor reported the theft to the congregation that assembled not long after. His voice trembled as he told them what he had found earlier that morning. For a person to steal the very symbol of their reason for celebrating, he said, their very reason for hope—well, he just did not understand. His gaze swept over the faces in the early morning congregation, disappointed to think someone in his own congregation might do such a thing.

  "The figure of the Christ Child," he said, "must be

returned before this Christmas Day is over. No one will ask any questions, but it must be brought back immediately." Then he slipped from the pulpit, and the choir closed the service with a Christmas hymn, "O Come, Let Us Adore Him."

The manger remained empty throughout the day. Toward the end of the afternoon, discouraged and heavy-hearted, the pastor took a walk through the wintry streets of the neighborhood. Ahead of him he saw one of the youngest members of his flock, a six-year-old boy named Tommy. Bundled shabbily against the cold, Tommy trudged up the sidewalk, proudly dragging behind him a toy express wagon. It was bright and red and obviously Christmas-new.

Knowing what sacrifice and scrimping the purchase of this toy must have meant—Tommy's family could barely make ends meet—the pastor was deeply touched. The love Tommy's parents had for their little boy gave the pastor's heart a gentle warmth, and he felt his faith in human nature beginning to return. He sped up so he could wish Tommy a merry Christmas and admire the beautiful new wagon.

But as he drew nearer he saw that the wagon was not empty—there lay the baby Jesus, now wrapped and blanketed but not quite hidden. The pastor crouched down beside Tommy, one knee feeling the damp snow through his pant leg. His face was grim and disappointed. Tommy may be just a little boy, and one must make allowances of course—but he was still old enough to understand that stealing was very wrong. The pastor made this crystal clear to Tommy while the little boy stood, his seemingly guiltless, clear eyes filling with what the pastor was sure were penitent tears.

"But, Pastor," the small boy quavered when at last the man finished talking, "I didn't *steal* Jesus. It wasn't like that at all." He paused to swallow hard and wipe a few tears away. "It's just that I've been asking Him for a red wagon as a Christmas present for a long time—and I promised Him that when I got it I'd take Him out for the first ride." ❊

Lord,

what wonderful blessings you have in store for us!

Please help us pray with expectation, fully trusting that you are in control.

In Jesus' name, amen.

✳

ALL HONOR TO THE GOD AND FATHER OF OUR

LORD JESUS CHRIST, FOR IT IS BY HIS BOUNDLESS MERCY THAT

GOD HAS GIVEN US THE PRIVILEGE OF BEING BORN AGAIN.

NOW WE LIVE WITH A WONDERFUL EXPECTATION BECAUSE

JESUS CHRIST ROSE AGAIN FROM THE DEAD.

I PETER I:3

SPEND AN EVENING SITTING IN FRONT OF YOUR

CHRISTMAS TREE, LISTENING TO CHRISTMAS MUSIC

BY CANDLELIGHT.

There's a reassuring comfort in the joy glad

tidings bring and an inner peace from honoring

and praising Christ the King.

JAN MILLER GIRANDO

CHAPTER 5

The Gift of Comfort

GOD REST YE MERRY, GENTLEMEN

English Traditional, Eighteenth Century

God rest ye merry, gentlemen,

Let nothing you dismay,

Remember Christ our Savior

Was born on Christmas Day;

To save us all from Satan's power

When we were gone astray.

O tidings of comfort and joy,

Comfort and joy,

O tidings of comfort and joy.

In Bethlehem, in Jewry,

This blessed Babe was born,

And laid within a manger,

Upon this blessed morn;

The which His mother Mary

Did nothing take in scorn.

From God our Heavenly Father,

A blessed angel came;

And unto certain shepherds

Brought tidings of the same:

How that in Bethlehem was born

The Son of God by Name.

"LET NOTHING YOU DISMAY."
What a seemingly impossible concept!
However, there is a reality in that statement
from the classic carol "God Rest Ye Merry,
Gentlemen"—a reality found only by
centering our lives on God and his eternal
perspective. No other comfort holds such
power for causing the concerns of this life
to fade in intensity.

When we take hold of God's offer
of salvation and promise of eternity with
him, our priorities are transformed and our
spirits are refreshed. When we make room
for Jesus, the dismaying circumstances in
life take on a whole new light. Yes, sickness
is still frightening, financial stresses don't
immediately disappear, and relationships
are not automatically mended. But through it
all, there is a Father who longs to hold you.

God's embrace becomes more dear
by the day. Why close the door on that
kind of comfort?

"LOOK! HERE I STAND AT THE DOOR AND KNOCK. IF YOU HEAR ME

CALLING AND OPEN THE DOOR, I WILL COME IN,

AND WE WILL SHARE A MEAL AS FRIENDS."

REVELATION 3:20

Trouble at the Inn

BY DINA DONOHUE

For years now whenever Christmas pageants are talked about in a certain little town in the Midwest, someone is sure to mention the name of Wallace Purling. Wally's performance in one annual production of the Nativity play has slipped into the realm of legend. But the old-timers who were in the audience that night never tire of recalling exactly what happened.

Wally was nine that year and in the second grade, though he should have been in the fourth. Most people in town knew that he had difficulty in keeping up. He was big and clumsy, slow in movement and mind. Still, Wally was well liked by the other children in his class, all of whom were smaller than he, though the boys had trouble hiding their irritation when the uncoordinated Wally would ask to play ball with them.

Most often they'd find a way to keep him off the field,

but Wally would hang around anyway—not sulking, just hoping. He was always a helpful boy, a willing and smiling one and the natural protector, paradoxically, of the underdog. Sometimes if the older boys chased the younger ones away, it would always be Wally who'd say, "Can't they stay? They're no bother."

Wally fancied the idea of being a shepherd with a flute in the Christmas pageant that year, but the play's director, Miss Lombard, assigned him to a more important role. After all, she reasoned, the Innkeeper did not have too many lines, and Wally's size would make his refusal of lodging to Joseph more forceful.

And so it happened that the usual large, partisan audience gathered for the town's Yuletide extravaganza of the crooks and creches, of beards, crowns, halos, and a whole stageful of squeaky voices. No one on stage or off was more caught up in the magic of the night than Wallace Purling. They said later that he stood in the wings and watched the performance with such fascination that from time to time Miss Lombard had to make sure he didn't wander onstage before his cue.

Then the time came when Joseph appeared, slowly, tenderly guiding Mary to the door of the inn. Joseph knocked hard on the wooden door set into the painted backdrop. Wally the Innkeeper was there waiting.

"What do you want?" Wally said, swinging the door open with a brusque gesture.

"We seek lodging."

"Seek it elsewhere." Wally looked straight ahead but spoke vigorously. "The inn is filled."

"Sir, we have asked everywhere in vain. We have traveled far and are very weary."

"There is no room in the inn for you." Wally looked properly stern.

"Please, good innkeeper, this is my wife, Mary. She is heavy with child and needs a place to rest. Surely you must have some small corner for her. She is so tired."

Now for the first time, the Innkeeper relaxed his stiff stance and looked down at Mary. With that, there was a long pause, long enough to make the audience a bit tense with embarrassment.

"No! Be gone!" the prompter whispered from the wings.

"No!" Wally repeated automatically. "Be gone!"

Joseph sadly placed his arm around Mary, and the two of them started to move away. The Innkeeper did not return inside his inn, however. Wally stood there in the doorway, watching the forlorn couple. His mouth was open, his brow creased with concern, his eyes filling unmistakably with tears.

And suddenly this Christmas pageant became different from all others.

"Don't go, Joseph," Wally called out. "Bring Mary back." And Wallace Purling's face grew into a bright smile. "You can have my room."

Some people in town thought that the pageant had been ruined. Yet there were others—many, many others—who considered it the most Christmassy of all Christmas pageants they had ever seen. ❄

Heavenly Father,

during this wonderful season of Christmas, we remember those who

may not be enjoying life right now. May you give them the abiding

comfort that comes only from you.

Amen.

*

MAY OUR LORD JESUS CHRIST AND GOD OUR FATHER,
WHO LOVED US AND IN HIS SPECIAL FAVOR GAVE US EVERLASTING
COMFORT AND GOOD HOPE, COMFORT YOUR HEARTS AND GIVE YOU
STRENGTH IN EVERY GOOD THING YOU DO AND SAY.

2 THESSALONIANS 2:16-17

READ THE BIBLE STORY OF THE FIRST CHRISTMAS.

(SEE LUKE 2:1-20.)

Treasured remembrances tug at our

heartstrings, bringing our past ever near. Keeping alive within

warm recollections family and friends we hold dear.

JAN MILLER GIRANDO

CHAPTER 6

The Gift of Memory

THE FIRST NOEL

English Traditional, Seventeenth Century

THE FIRST NOEL THE ANGEL DID SAY

WAS TO CERTAIN POOR SHEPHERDS IN FIELDS AS THEY LAY;

IN FIELDS WHERE THEY LAY KEEPING THEIR SHEEP

ON A COLD WINTER'S NIGHT THAT WAS SO DEEP.

NOEL, NOEL, NOEL, NOEL,

BORN IS THE KING OF ISRAEL!

THEY LOOKED UP AND SAW A STAR

SHINING IN THE EAST BEYOND THEM FAR,

AND TO THE EARTH IT GAVE GREAT LIGHT,

AND SO IT CONTINUED BOTH DAY AND NIGHT.

THEN LET US ALL WITH ONE ACCORD

SING PRAISES TO OUR HEAVENLY LORD;

THAT HATH MADE HEAVEN AND EARTH OF NAUGHT

AND WITH HIS BLOOD MANKIND HATH BOUGHT.

EACH LIFETIME HAS ITS SHARE of "firsts." First steps in babyhood, first day of school, first best friend, first heartache . . .

Jesus' birth two thousand years ago marked a huge "first" for more than just the growing family he was born into. Life on earth would never be the same again. From the moment God entered the world as a baby, every life was given the opportunity to know God in a personal way.

The first Christmas is a memory to be cherished, and "The First Noel" celebrates that gift and acknowledges that the greatest gifts are yet to come. Abundant life is ready to be lived because of one memorable day so long ago.

I RECALL ALL YOU HAVE DONE, O LORD;

I REMEMBER YOUR WONDERFUL DEEDS OF LONG AGO.

PSALM 77:11

And for as Long as I Can Remember

BY CATHERINE OTTEN

Mama wasn't stingy—far from it—but I never saw her spend a dime. When we were young, I suppose we didn't notice her thrifty quirk, but as we grew up, we all worried about Mama's concern with dimes.

Mama ran our house like a tight little ship. She and Papa set the course for their young crew, which was made up of my two sisters, my two brothers, and me.

The term "good old days" could have originated in our home. Mama never ran out of energy or food and we seldom ate Sunday suppers alone. Unexpected company usually dropped in, and there was always enough food to go around—Mama's Saturday baking binge took care of that. Little did we youngsters know or care that those were the days of the Depression. But we never felt deprived.

Years slipped by, and one by one we left home to start families of our own. When Papa retired, he and Mama moved into our summer cottage.

During our visits, we became more aware of Mama's obsession with dimes. When we shopped with her, she refused to use a single dime, even if it meant breaking a dollar bill to pay for a ten-cent item. What was wrong with our mother?

Christmas was the time we all gathered for a big family dinner. Mama would have it no other way.

"Dinner is at four o'clock," Mama would say. "Just bring yourselves, and don't be late."

Dad would be busy for weeks making wreaths from the pine trees in the yard. One Christmas every window boasted a small wreath, and a huge one decorated the door.

By the time the last family arrived with their treasures, the pile of gifts resembled a pyramid, competing in height and beauty with the shining Christmas tree.

The Christmas dinner table was another picture that we shall never forget. It had been pulled out into the living room, and stretched to its full length. The shining dishes and silverware had been polished to the hilt for the occasion.

The centerpiece was always the same—little wax candle

skaters, snowmen, angels, animals, and trees carefully placed on the raised round reflector. The sparkling wine glasses and water goblets resembled a picket fence around the relish dishes, salads, cranberries, biscuits, mints, and nuts.

The hot dishes were brought in with ceremony. The huge, golden-brown turkey was placed in front of Papa. Then came platters of buttery vegetables and heaping bowls of mashed and sweet potatoes. Papa led grace as our eyes feasted on the picture before us. We toasted everyone's welfare in the coming year, and the feast began.

One Christmas, as we put away the dishes and the left-overs, we girls ganged up on Mama and insisted on sharing the expenses of the day. She was quiet for a bit, and then she revealed her secret.

"Don't worry children," she laughed. "I pay for it all with a year of dimes that I've saved."

We looked at each other guiltily. Our concern over Mama's thing with dimes melted into relief. The joke was on us!

Years have passed since that Christmas. Now my children are grown and raising families of their own, passing on the giving-traditions that our parents gave to us.

Father God,

we rejoice in the season of your Son's birth!

By your grace may we always remember how dearly you

paid for our salvation.

Through Jesus we pray, amen.

＊

WHO CAN FORGET THE WONDERS HE PERFORMS?

HOW GRACIOUS AND MERCIFUL IS OUR LORD!

PSALM 111:4

ON A SMALL PIECE OF PAPER, WRITE A CURRENT

CONCERN IN YOUR LIFE. ROLL IT UP AND PUT IT IN A

SMALL PIECE OF NETTING ALONG WITH SOME POTPOURRI.

TIE IT UP WITH A RIBBON AND HANG IT ON

YOUR CHRISTMAS TREE TO SYMBOLIZE AN OFFERING

YOU ARE GIVING TO GOD. MAKE A CONSCIOUS EFFORT

TO BE FREE FROM WORRY, TRUSTING THAT YOUR

CONCERN IS IN HIS HANDS.

Christ is the only liberator whose liberation

lasts forever.

MALCOLM MUGGERIDGE

The Gift of Freedom

57

James Montgomery, 1816

ANGELS FROM THE REALMS OF GLORY,

WING YOUR FLIGHT O'ER ALL THE EARTH;

YE WHO SANG CREATION'S STORY,

NOW PROCLAIM MESSIAH'S BIRTH:

COME AND WORSHIP, COME AND WORSHIP,

WORSHIP CHRIST, THE NEWBORN KING.

SHEPHERDS, IN THE FIELD ABIDING,

WATCHING O'ER YOUR FLOCKS BY NIGHT,

GOD WITH MAN IS NOW RESIDING,

YONDER SHINES THE INFANT LIGHT:

SAGES, LEAVE YOUR CONTEMPLATIONS,

BRIGHTER VISIONS BEAM AFAR;

SEEK THE GREAT DESIRE OF NATIONS,

YE HAVE SEEN HIS NATAL STAR.

THE GIFT OF FREEDOM IS EASY TO take for granted. The magnitude of its worth cannot be completely understood unless one has personally experienced life without it.

In the history of the world, freedom has never come cheaply. Individuals have dreamed of it, nations have battled over it, and God went to the greatest possible lengths to free each one of us.

Generations of Israelites had prayed and waited for God to fulfill his promise of a Messiah who would bring freedom from the tyranny of the Roman Empire. Fortunately for all of humanity, God saw our far greater need for spiritual freedom. His response was that of an all-powerful, unconditionally loving Father.

Jesus' birth was just the beginning of his mission on earth. He came to take on the greatest bondage so we could experience the greatest freedom. As the song later states, "Justice now revokes the sentence, Mercy calls you, break your chains."

WHEREVER THE SPIRIT OF THE LORD IS, HE GIVES FREEDOM.

2 CORINTHIANS 3:17

Adapted from "The Dime"

AUTHOR UNKNOWN

Bobby was getting cold sitting out in his backyard in the snow. He didn't wear boots—he didn't like them, and he didn't own any. The thin sneakers he wore had a few holes in them, and they did a poor job of keeping out the cold. Bobby had been in his backyard for about an hour. Try as he might, he could not come up with an idea for his mother's Christmas gift. He shook his head as he thought, "This is useless. Even if I do come up with an idea, I don't have any money to spend."

Ever since his father had passed away three years ago, the family of five had struggled. It wasn't because his mother didn't care, or try, there just never seemed to be enough. She worked nights at the hospital, but the small wage that she brought home could only be stretched so far. The riches the family possessed were those of the heart instead of the pocketbook.

Bobby had three sisters—two older and one younger—who ran the household in their mother's absence. His sisters had already made beautiful gifts for their mother. Somehow it just wasn't fair. It was Christmas Eve, and he had nothing.

Wiping a tear from his eye, Bobby kicked the snow and started to walk down to the street where the shops and stores were. It wasn't easy being six without a father, especially when he needed a man to talk to. Bobby walked from shop to shop, looking into each decorated window. Everything seemed so beautiful and so out of reach.

It was starting to get dark, and Bobby reluctantly turned to walk home. Suddenly his eyes caught the glimmer of the setting sun's rays reflecting off of something along the curb. He reached down and discovered a shiny dime. Never before has anyone felt so wealthy as Bobby did at that moment. As he held his newfound treasure, a warmth spread throughout his entire body, and he walked into the first store he saw.

His excitement quickly turned cold when the salesperson told him that he couldn't buy anything with only a dime. He noticed a flower shop and went inside to wait in line. When the shop owner asked if he could help him, Bobby presented the dime and asked if he could buy one flower for his mother's Christmas gift. The shop owner looked at Bobby and his ten-cent offering. Then he put his hand on Bobby's shoulder and said to him, "You just wait here and I'll see what I can do for you."

As Bobby waited, he looked at all the beautiful flowers and could see why mothers and girls liked flowers. The sound of the door closing as the last customer left jolted Bobby back to reality. All alone in the shop, Bobby began to feel alone and afraid. Suddenly the shop owner came out and moved to the counter. There, before Bobby's eyes, lay twelve long stem, red roses, with leaves of green and tiny white flowers all tied together with a big silver bow.

Bobby's heart sank as the owner picked them up and placed them neatly into a long, white box. "That will be ten cents, young man," the shop owner said, reaching out his hand for the dime. Slowly, Bobby moved his hand to give the man his dime. Could this be true? No one else would give him a thing for his dime!

Sensing the boy's reluctance, the shop owner added, "I just happened to have some roses on sale for ten cents a dozen. Would you like them?" This time Bobby did not hesitate, and when the man placed the long box into his hands, he knew it was true. Walking out the door that the owner was holding open for him, Bobby heard the shopkeeper say, "Merry Christmas, son."

As the shopkeeper returned inside, the shopkeeper's wife walked out. "Who were you talking to back there and where are the roses you were fixing?"

Staring out the window and blinking the tears from his own eyes, he replied, "A strange thing happened to me this morning. While I was setting up things to open the shop, I thought I heard a voice telling me to set aside a dozen of my best roses for a special gift. I wasn't sure at the time whether I had lost my mind, but I set them aside anyway. Just a few minutes ago, a little boy came into the shop and wanted to buy a flower for his mother with one small dime.

"When I looked at him, I saw myself, many years ago. I, too, was a poor boy having nothing with which to buy my mother

a Christmas gift. A bearded man, whom I had never known, stopped me on the street and told me that he wanted to give me ten dollars.

"When I saw that little boy tonight, I knew I needed to put together a dozen of my very best roses."

The shop owner and his wife hugged each other tightly, remembering anew the true freedom of the season of giving. ❄

Lord,

remind us each day, just how free we are in you.

Don't let us take for granted the magnitude of the soul-freedom you

made possible through Jesus' life and death.

Amen.

✳

GOD ALONE MADE IT POSSIBLE FOR YOU TO BE

IN CHRIST JESUS. FOR OUR BENEFIT GOD MADE CHRIST TO

BE WISDOM ITSELF. HE IS THE ONE WHO MADE US

ACCEPTABLE TO GOD. HE MADE US PURE AND HOLY, AND HE

GAVE HIMSELF TO PURCHASE OUR FREEDOM.

I CORINTHIANS 1:30

TIE A RIBBON TO THE CHRISTMAS TREE FOR EACH

MEMBER OF YOUR FAMILY; WRITE A LETTER TELLING

EACH ONE WHAT YOU FIND SPECIAL ABOUT HIM OR HER.

To get the full value of joy, we must have

somebody to divide it with.

MARK TWAIN

CHAPTER 8

The Gift of Relationship

67

O COME, ALL YE FAITHFUL

Latin, Eighteenth Century

O come, all ye faithful, joyful and triumphant,

O come ye, O come ye to Bethlehem!

Come and behold Him, born the King of angels!

O come, let us adore Him,

O come, let us adore Him,

O come, let us adore Him,

Christ the Lord!

Sing, choirs of angels, sing in exultation,

O sing, all ye citizens of heaven above!

Glory to God, glory in the highest!

Yea, Lord, we greet Thee, born this happy morning;

Jesus, to Thee be all glory given;

Word of the Father, now in flesh appearing!

WHAT VALUE WOULD THE OTHER gifts be without the wondrous gift of relationship alongside them? It's in the friendships and family ties that memories are made, love is shared, and hopes are nourished. And it was for the restoration of relationships that God sent his Son, Jesus, to earth.

"O Come, All Ye Faithful" is a call to join in the rejoicing about the Savior's birth. The joy born that night is evidenced today by everyone who acknowledges the true meaning of the season. For those households that center the holiday festivities on Jesus' birth, normal troubles and stresses of daily life diminish in intensity amidst the hope and truth of Christmas.

God's enduring love radiates through the world today. Let us sing with gratitude, as a later verse of the song states, "Who would not love thee, loving us so dearly?"

WE CAN REJOICE IN OUR WONDERFUL NEW RELATIONSHIP WITH GOD—ALL BECAUSE OF WHAT OUR LORD JESUS CHRIST HAS DONE FOR US IN MAKING US FRIENDS OF GOD.

ROMANS 5:11

Christmas Is for Love

AUTHOR UNKNOWN

Christmas is for love. It is for joy, for giving and sharing, for laughter, for reuniting with family and friends, for tinsel and brightly decorated packages. But mostly, Christmas is for love. I had not believed this until a small elf-like student with wide, innocent eyes and soft rosy cheeks gave me a wondrous gift one Christmas.

Mark was an eleven-year-old orphan who lived with his aunt, a bitter middle-aged woman greatly annoyed with the burden of caring for her dead sister's son. She never failed to remind young Mark, if it hadn't been for her generosity, he would be a vagrant, homeless waif. Still, with all the scolding and chilliness at home, he was a sweet and gentle child.

I had not noticed Mark particularly until he began staying after class each day (at the risk of arousing his aunt's anger, I later found) to help me straighten up the room. We did this quietly and comfortably, not speaking much, but enjoying the solitude of that hour of the day. When we did talk, Mark spoke mostly of his mother. Though he was quite small when she died, he remembered a kind, gentle, loving woman who always spent much time with him.

As Christmas drew near however, Mark failed to stay after school each day. I looked forward to his coming, and when the days passed and he continued to scamper hurriedly from the room after class, I stopped him one afternoon and asked why he no longer helped me in the room. I told him how I had missed him, and his large gray eyes lit up eagerly as he replied, "Did you really miss me?"

I explained how he had been my best helper. "I was making you a surprise," he whispered confidentially. "It's for Christmas." With that, he became embarrassed and dashed from the room. He didn't stay after school anymore after that.

Finally came the last school day before Christmas. Mark crept slowly into the room late that afternoon with his hands concealing something behind his back. "I have your present," he said timidly when I looked up. "I hope you like it." He held out his hands, and there lying in his small palms was a tiny wooden box.

"It's beautiful, Mark. Is there something in it?" I asked, opening the top to look inside.

"Oh, you can't see what's in it," he replied, "and you can't touch it or taste it or feel it. But Mother always said it makes you feel good all the time, warm on cold nights, and safe when you're all alone."

I gazed into the empty box. "What is it, Mark," I asked gently, "that will make me feel so good?"

"It's love," he whispered softly, "and Mother always said it's best when you give it away." And he turned and quietly left the room.

So now I keep a small box crudely made of scraps of wood on the piano in my living room and only smile as inquiring friends raise quizzical eyebrows when I explain to them that there is love in it.

Yes, Christmas is for gaiety, mirth, and song—for good and wondrous gifts. But mostly, Christmas is for love. ❈

Almighty God,

you have so many names that describe your relationship to us.

During the upcoming year, grant us a more complete sense of you as our

heavenly Father, provider, friend, and Savior.

Amen.

✳

DEAR FRIENDS, SINCE GOD LOVED US THAT MUCH,

WE SURELY OUGHT TO LOVE EACH OTHER.

1 JOHN 4:11

TREAT YOURSELF TO A REFRESHING,

CANDLELIT BUBBLE BATH.

Love alone could waken love.

PEARL S. BUCK

CHAPTER 9

The Gift of Refreshment

IT CAME UPON A MIDNIGHT CLEAR

Edmund H. Sears, 1850

It came upon a midnight clear,
That glorious song of old,
From angels bending near the earth
To touch their harps of gold;
Peace on the earth, good will to men
From heaven's all-gracious King.
The world in solemn stillness lay
To hear the angels sing.

Still through the cloven skies they come,
With peaceful wings unfurled;
And still their heavenly music floats
O'er all the weary world;
Above its sad and lowly plains
They bend on hovering wing,
And ever o'er its Babel sounds
The blessed angels sing.

For lo! The days are hast'ning on,
By prophets seen of old,
When with the ever-circling years
Shall come the time foretold,
When peace shall over all the earth
Its ancient splendors fling,
And the whole world give back the song
Which now the angels sing.

THE NATIVITY IS AN IMAGE THAT has been burned into our minds from childhood. How familiar it is at Christmas to imagine a brilliant star lighting up the earth and thousands of angels rejoicing as they hover over a crude stable.

For the few who recognized who Jesus was and what his life would mean for them, that first Christmas night most certainly brought an overwhelming sense of refreshment and awe.

The classic carol "It Came upon a Midnight Clear" beautifully recalls the scene of a world weary from toil and discouragement being awakened by a sky alight with the glory of God. Speaking to those beneath life's crushing load, the songwriter unveils a wonderful image of future joy: "When peace shall over all the earth its ancient splendors fling, and the whole world give back the song which now the angels sing"!

Knowing the Savior promises refreshment beyond anyone's most heartfelt hopes.

WONDERFUL TIMES OF REFRESHMENT WILL COME

FROM THE PRESENCE OF THE LORD.

ACTS 3:20

Adapted from "The Doll and a White Rose"

By V. A. Bailey

Hurrying into the local department store to grab some last-minute Christmas gifts, I looked at all the people and grumbled to myself. I would be in here forever and I had so much to do! Christmas was becoming such a drag—I wished I could just sleep through it all. But I hurried the best I could to the toy department. Once again I mumbled to myself at the toy prices and wondered if the grandkids would even play with them.

In the doll aisle I saw a little boy about five holding a lovely doll. He held her so gently and kept touching her hair. I wondered who the doll was for as I watched him turn to a woman nearby. Calling his aunt by name, he said, "Are you sure I don't have enough money?"

She replied a bit impatiently, "You know you don't have enough money for it. Now don't go anywhere. I have to get some other things, but I'll be back in a few minutes." And then she left the aisle.

Approaching the boy, I asked him who the doll was for.

"It's the doll my sister wanted so badly for Christmas. She just knew Santa would bring it."

I told him maybe Santa would do just that.

"No," he replied, "Santa can't go where my sister is. I have to give the doll to my momma to take to her."

I asked him where his sister was. He looked at me with the saddest eyes and said, "She has gone to be with Jesus. My daddy says that Momma is going to be with her."

My heart nearly stopped beating. The boy looked at me again and said, "I told Daddy to tell Momma not to go yet. I told him to tell her to wait till I got back from the store."

He pulled out a picture he had taken at the front of the store and said, "I want my momma to take this with her so she don't ever forget me. I love my momma so much, and I wish she didn't have to leave me. But Daddy says she will need to be with my sister."

The little boy had lowered his head and grew very quiet. While he wasn't looking I reached into my purse and pulled out a handful of bills. "Shall we count that money one more time?"

He grew excited and said, "Yes, I just know it has to be enough!" So I slipped my money in with his and we began to count it. And of course it was plenty for the doll. He softly said,

"Thank you, Jesus, for giving me enough money."

The boy continued, "I just asked Jesus to give me enough money to buy this doll so Momma can take it with her to give to my sister. And he heard my prayer. I wanted to ask him for enough to buy my momma a white rose, but I didn't ask him, but he gave me enough to buy the doll and a rose for Momma. She loves white roses so very much."

After a few minutes the aunt came back and I wheeled my cart away. I thought about the little boy as I finished my shopping in a totally different spirit than when I had started. And I kept remembering a newspaper story several days earlier about a drunk driver hitting a car and killing a little girl, leaving the mother in serious condition. The family was deciding whether to remove the life support. Surely this little boy did not belong with that story. . . .

Two days later I read in the paper that the family had disconnected the life support and the young woman had died. I couldn't forget the little boy and wondered if the two were somehow connected. Later that day I went out and bought some white roses and took them to the funeral home where the young woman was. And there she was holding a lovely white rose, the beautiful doll, and the picture of the little boy in the store.

And I now held in my heart the true spirit of giving. ❄

Lord God,

thank you for the peace you brought to the earth on

the night of Jesus' birth—may we experience that more

and more as we seek your heart.

Amen.

✳

"I AM LEAVING YOU WITH A GIFT—PEACE OF MIND AND HEART.

AND THE PEACE I GIVE ISN'T LIKE THE PEACE THE WORLD GIVES.

SO DON'T BE TROUBLED OR AFRAID."

JOHN 14:27

TAKE A DRIVE DOWN A COUNTRY LANE AND

APPRECIATE THE PEACE AND QUIET.

Peace was the first thing the angels sang.

Peace is the mark of the sons of God. Peace is the nurse of love.

Peace is the mother of unity. Peace is the rest of blessed souls.

Peace is the dwelling place of eternity.

POPE LEO THE GREAT

CHAPTER 10

The Gift of Peace

SILENT NIGHT

Joseph Mohr, 1818

SILENT NIGHT, HOLY NIGHT,

ALL IS CALM, ALL IS BRIGHT;

ROUND YON VIRGIN MOTHER AND CHILD,

HOLY INFANT, SO TENDER AND MILD,

SLEEP IN HEAVENLY PEACE,

SLEEP IN HEAVENLY PEACE.

SILENT NIGHT, HOLY NIGHT,

SHEPHERDS QUAKE AT THE SIGHT,

GLORIES STREAM FROM HEAVEN AFAR,

HEAVENLY HOSTS SING, ALLELUIA!

CHRIST, THE SAVIOR, IS BORN!

CHRIST, THE SAVIOR, IS BORN!

SILENT NIGHT, HOLY NIGHT,

SON OF GOD, LOVE'S PURE LIGHT,

RADIANT BEAMS FROM THY HOLY FACE,

WITH THE DAWN OF REDEEMING GRACE,

JESUS, LORD, AT THY BIRTH,

JESUS, LORD, AT THY BIRTH.

PEACE IS THE LASTING SENSE OF serenity we all long for. Not dependent on circumstances, it keeps us calm and secure amidst the storms of life.

God is the one true source of peace, and it's through his Son, Jesus, that we can experience all that his peace truly is. The same God who came to earth as a tiny baby is still alive and working today. And the message of the song "Silent Night" rings true even among the chaos and hardships that fill the world.

The same God who created the mountains and meadows, rivers and oceans, chose to give up everything to rescue us. His gifts of life, love, and relationship provided for us a salvation beyond what we knew we needed. And a true, abiding relationship with him brings with it the comfort, refreshment, and freedom of his abiding peace.

His heart was broken over our need for him. That's the miraculous gift of Christmas.

MAY THE LORD OF PEACE HIMSELF ALWAYS GIVE YOU HIS PEACE NO MATTER WHAT HAPPENS.

2 THESSALONIANS 3:16

Unexpected Christmas

BY MARGUERITE NIXON

What can one do when a torrential storm closes off home, and one is forced to spend Christmas Eve with strangers . . . strangers who have so very little . . . just a rather poor farm . . . and some animals in a barn?

We were well over halfway to our farm in East Texas when the storm broke. Lightning flashed, thunder crashed, and a tree fell with a great ripping noise. When the rain poured in such a flood that we could not see the road, my husband drove off onto what seemed to be a bit of clearing deep in the piney woods.

As we waited I sensed we would not get to the farm that night to celebrate Christmas Eve with our family. We were sitting there, miserable and dejected, when I heard a knocking on my window. A man with a lantern stood there, beckoning us to follow him. My husband and I splashed after him up the path to his house.

A woman with a lamp in her hand stood in the doorway of an old house; a boy of about twelve, and a little girl stood beside her. We went in, soaked and dripping, and the family moved aside so we might have the warmth of the fire. With the volubility of city people, my husband and I began to talk, explaining our plans. And with the quietness of people who live in the silence of the woods, they listened.

"The bridge on Caney Creek is out. You are welcome to spend the night with us," the man said. And though we told them we thought it was an imposition, especially on Christmas Eve, they insisted. After we had visited a while longer, the man got up and took the Bible from the mantel. "It's our custom to read the Bible story from Luke on Christmas Eve," he said, and without another word he began.

"'And she brought forth her firstborn Son, and wrapped Him in swaddling clothes, and laid Him in a manger.'"

The children sat up eagerly, their eyes bright in anticipation, while their father read on.

"'And there were in the same country shepherds abiding in

the field, keeping watch over their flocks by night.'"

I looked at his strong face. He could have been one of them. When he finished reading and closed the Bible, the little children knelt by their chairs. The mother and father were kneeling and, without any conscious will of my own, I found myself joining them. Then I saw my husband, without any embarrassment at all, kneel also.

When we arose, I looked around the room. There were no brightly-wrapped packages or cards, only a small, unadorned holly tree on the mantel. Yet the spirit of Christmas was never more real to me.

The little boy broke the silence. "We always feed the cattle at 12:00 on Christmas Eve. Come with us."

The barn was warm and fragrant with the smell of hay and dried corn. A cow and a horse greeted us, and there was a goat with a tiny, woolly kid that came up to be petted. *This is like the stable where the baby Jesus was born,* I thought. *Here is the manger, and the gentle animals keep watch.*

When we returned to the house, there was an air of

festivity and the serving of juice and fruitcake. Later, we bedded down on a mattress made of corn shucks. As I turned into a comfortable position, they rustled under me and sent up a faint fragrance exactly like that in the barn. My heart said, *You are sleeping in the stable like the Christ child did.* As I drifted into a profound sleep, I knew that the light coming through the old pine shutters was the star shining on that quiet house.

The family all walked down the path to the car with us the next morning. I was so filled with the Spirit of Christmas they had given me that I could find no words. Suddenly I thought of the gifts in the back seat of our car for our family.

I began to hand them out. My husband's gray woolen socks went to the man. The red sweater I had bought for my sister went to the mother. I gave away two boxes of candy, the white mittens, and the leather gloves while my husband nodded approval.

And when I was breathless from reaching in and out of the car and the family stood there loaded with the gaiety of Christmas packages, the mother spoke for all of them. "We thank you," she said simply. And then she said, "Wait."

She hurried up the path to the house and came back with a quilt folded across her arms. It was beautifully handmade; the pattern was the Star of Bethlehem. I looked up at the tall beautiful pines because my throat hurt and I could not speak. It was indeed Christmas.

Every Christmas Eve since then I sleep under the quilt, the Star of Bethlehem, and in memory I visit the stable and smell again the corn shucks, and the meaning of Christmas abides with me once more. ❧

Lord God,

thank you for the peace you brought to the earth

on the night of Jesus' birth—may we experience that more

and more as we seek your heart.

Amen.

*

"I AM LEAVING YOU WITH A GIFT—
PEACE OF MIND AND HEART. AND THE PEACE I GIVE
ISN'T LIKE THE PEACE THE WORLD GIVES.
SO DON'T BE TROUBLED OR AFRAID."

JOHN 14:27